S0-BXK-121

SWAMP SONG

STANLEY BURKE * ROY PETERSON

Douglas & McIntyre
Vancouver

Text copyright © Stanley Burke, 1978
Drawings copyright © Roy Peterson, 1978

All rights reserved. No part of this book may be
reproduced or transmitted in any form or by any
means without permission in writing from the
publisher, except by a reviewer, who may quote
brief passages in a review.

Canadian Cataloguing in Publication Data

Burke, Stanley, 1923-
    Swamp song

ISBN 0-88894-212-5

  1. Canada — Politics and government —
1963-   Anecdotes, facetiae, satire, etc.
I. Peterson, Roy.   II. Title.
FC173.B873   971.06'44'0207   C78-002177-0
F1034.2.B873

Cover design by Roy Peterson
Design co-ordination by Ian Bateson
Typesetting by Frebo Studio Limited

Douglas & McIntyre Ltd.
1875 Welch Street
North Vancouver, British Columbia

Printed and bound in Canada by Hunter Rose

The Swamp was going down the drain.

Unemployment was higher than the food prices at E.P. Tailer's Super-Markup, while the Swampian unit of currency, instead of floating, had sunk. René Terrifique was making off with the Shallow End of the Swamp, the Otters and Marmots were stealing the west, and at the Swampian Bureau of Statistics, Sylvia Ostrich's figures showed that it was time to bail out.

In the capital at Nottalot, Peter Waterhole wondered how it had all happened. "It was not like this in the old days," he said sadly. "The animals used to work hard and make clams and everyone was happy."

On the other side of Nottalot, Joe Hoo, the Befuddled Owl, also wondered. He knew, of course, that it was all the fault of Peter Waterhole and his friends, but he was equally uncertain as to what to do about it.

"Waterhole is wallowing," he told the animals. "Elect me and I'll think of something."

Joe Hoo, you see, was the Leader of the Supposition, so named because of the supposition that everything about the government was wrong. No matter what the government did, Joe Hoo's job was to stand up and say how bad it was, although in the stillness of his heart he was as confused as Peter Waterhole.

What had gone wrong? Why had the Swamp changed?

In the days of the first inhabitants, the Turtles, the animals had sung and danced and, close to nature, lived happy, hardy lives.

Then the Frogs came and conquered the Turtles and made long, brave voyages of discovery and sang and danced and they, too, lived wonderful lives.

Then the Beavers conquered both the Frogs and the Turtles. They were odd animals, however, who did not sing and dance and who took pleasure only in building their wonderful dam. This dam benefitted the other animals, so for a time they all lived happily enough together — except that the Frogs and Turtles, being emotional, could not forget being conquered. The Beavers said this was unreasonable.

"We don't hold grudges," said the sensible Beavers. "Why should they?"

But the other animals were not sensible, and as time went by they began to grumble more and more.

There were the unhappy lobsters who dwelt far to the east, beyond the Shallow End where the Frogs lived. Once they had been rich but, having joined the Beavers, they were now poor. Still, they remained loyal to the Beavers' dream and believed that somehow hard work would make things better — even if there was no work to do.

In the Meadowland to the west lived the Gophers, who worked industriously gathering seeds which were sold for them by the Beavers. This, they noticed, made for many rich Beavers but few rich Gophers.

At the beginning of the Great Western Hills dwelt the Marmots, who worked hard digging holes from which flowed wonderful stuff called Swamp Oil. This Swamp Oil was much valued by the other creatures, and made the Marmots the richest of animals. Still they were not happy, because if it had not been for the Beavers and their price controls, they would have been richer still.

"Furthermore," said the Marmots "what will happen when the Swamp Oil is gone? We will be poor but the Beavers will be as rich as ever."

Finally, to the west of the Great Hills, lived the Otters, who caught fish and played and were happy — except when the Beavers cut their water off. Like the Lobsters, they had been uncertain about the Beavers from the beginning, but nevertheless remained loyal — well, fairly loyal — to the dream.

But, though they grumbled, all the animals agreed that the Swamp was wonderful and that, on the whole, life was good.

Far to the north, however, in a place called Rush-Ya, there dwelt evil animals called Come-You-Nits who wished to spoil all this. The Come-You-Nits, like their friends the Social-Lusts, did not believe in hard work and said that instead it was easier to take from the rich and give to the poor.

This idea, though appealing, never really caught on with the rich, who were called Capital-Nits.

It particularly bothered the wealthy Eagles who lived to the south. Above all, it worried the Rocky Fellers, the richest of all Eagles.

"What we need," said the Rocky Fellers, "is a politician who is radical — but not too radical."

"And without too much charisma," said their public relations animal.

At that very moment, in walked a funny, fat little Beaver saying "Work if necessary, but not necessarily work" and "Happiness is doing as little as possible for as much as possible."

"Sign him!" cried the Rocky Fellers.

So, well financed, the funny little Beaver, whose name was William Lyin Mackenzie Sting, wrote an unreadable radical book and returned to the Swamp, where he invented the Gliberal Party and quickly became Chief Minister.

This splendid party was run by public-spirited creatures called Bag-Animals* who rallied the animals behind their noble cause.

The Great Animals were told that they could continue to own the Swamp and work as hard as they liked and become almost as rich as the Rocky Fellers.

The Ordinary Animals were told that they could get fairly rich without working at all, simply by voting Gliberal.

"What could be fairer than that?" asked the Bag-Animals.

Working together with the Bag-Animals were the wonderfully clever Civil Serpents who, coiled in their nests at Nottalot, could strike swiftly and decisively to see that the system worked the way they wanted it to.

*from the Frog *bagatelle* (a game played for low stakes), since the Gliberal patriots worked almost without pay.

Under them were the useful Bureaucrabs, so called because of their ability to make progress while going sideways.

At the bottom were the Snivel Servants who worked hard filling out birch bark forms on which they reported to the Bureaucrabs. The Bureaucrabs in turn made out more birch bark forms which they sent to the Civil Serpents, who filed them.

The purpose of this system was to see that the Swamp was well administered on behalf of the Ordinary Animals, who were incapable of doing anything for themselves.

These Civil Serpents and Bureaucrabs and Snivel Servants were vital to the Swamp, but more important still were the leaders of noble organizations called Bunions.* The Bunions were responsible for the creation of happiness itself through the abolition of work. This was accomplished through strict rules which ensured that, for example, no animal cut down more than one tree a day or caught more than one fish, and animals who disobeyed were severely, though democratically, punished.

"Some day," said the Bunion Bosses, "the scourge of work will be eradicated."

To further this aim, they invented annual Contract Negotiations, so named because at these times the bosses on both sides took out contracts on one another. During these negotiations, the Bunions would present their Just Demands, asking "just for this" and "just for that."

The Bunions would also, from time to time, declare long holidays called strikes which were intended to prepare the animals for the great day when work would vanish. During these holidays the members had all kinds of fun and sang songs about how fine it would be when no one did anything. One of the most famous of these was appropriately called "We Shall Not Be Moved."

In the length and frequency of the holidays, the Swamp led all the world and, in fact, became so advanced that it was difficult to tell whether the animals were on strike or not.

*because they were so hard and painful for the Capital-Nits who had them.

So for the Bunion Bosses life had finally become good and they could smile and enjoy the fruits of their labours. Perhaps the most rewarding thing of all was to see how much the Capital-Nits had learned and to realize that it was possible to sit with these once-evil animals on the same Boreds of Directors and even to join the same clubs.

In all this, however, one thing still bothered the Bunion Bosses, and this was the introduction of machines.

"Some day," said the Capital-Nits, "everything will be done by wonderful wooden machines and no one will work and everyone will consume."

"But when no one works, who will belong to the Bunions?" asked the Bunion Bosses.

"Everyone!" replied their researchers, who knew everything. "We will organize everything. We will organize the machines. We will organize the world!"

"The workers' paradise!" exclaimed the Bunion Bosses. "No one will work and everyone will be organized."

The Civil Serpents, too, dreamed dreams of paradise: a Swamp so perfectly administered that the happy animals would no longer concern themselves with things they did not understand and would leave everything to the Civil Serpents.

Alas, the Ordinary Animals denied the Civil Serpents the clams they needed to accomplish this, and then added insult to injury by accusing them of wastefulness. "If only we could get rid of the Ordinary Animals," said the Civil Serpents.

"Indeed," said the Capital-Nits and Bunion Bosses, for they too found the Ordinary Animals dense and difficult.

All at once they hit on a plan. "We will educate them," they exclaimed, "and soon there will be no more Ordinary Animals."

So the Civil Serpents created fascinating places called schools run by wise animals called Yackademics. These schools were cleverly designed to look and feel like factories, because the far-sighted Yackademics knew that, until work was eradicated, it would be necessary for the young to become used to employment in the Swamp's factory-lodges.

The Yackademics saw to it that their pupils even had their own Bunions, called student councils, so they could bargain for better leisure conditions. In fact, in the fight to eradicate work the schools led all the Swamp, and the Yackademics could proudly say, "Some day the Swamp will be as progressive as we are."

All of this reflected the wonderful system of Swampian democracy, and the Gliberal Bag-Animals looked on their creation and found it good.

"We will be re-elected forever," they told each other. "It's logical."

So it seemed until the days of Peter Waterhole, when, for some reason, the Swamp began to come apart.

Peter Waterhole could not understand it. He had come to power as the most confident Chief Minister the Swamp had ever known, and faithfully he had applied the magic Gliberal formula. But it no longer worked.

The animals were not happy, not grateful, and not united. Furthermore, some were getting hungry.

"I do everything right," he said in exasperation, "but the Swamp fuddles it up." Why? Had he not spent more of the Swamp's money than all previous Chief Ministers combined? "If that won't buy happiness, what will?" he demanded.

Why was the Swamp not united?

Had he not given two billion clams to Keith Spicy to teach the Swamp to speak Frog? Was it his fault if the idiot Beavers could not learn? And why were the Frogs not grateful anyhow?

Had he not appointed Jean Cretin as Finance Minister to prove that Frogs could spend money? Was he to blame if the Swamp could not understand Cretin's brilliant plans, which saved clams and spent them and created them, all at the same time? And at the Treasury Bored, had not Robert Undress explained with sheer genius how Less could be More? Why could the stupid animals not understand?

No one could tell him, not even the members of the Privvy Chamber, his personal staff, who were the most amazing collection of brains the Swamp had ever known. The Keeper of the Privvy was the brilliant Michael Pitstop, who came from a distinguished financial family and knew all about bottom lines. To the seats of power he had appointed a line-up of animals with a grasp of every aspect of Swampian life. But even these grasping animals were unable to tell Peter Waterhole what was wrong. Indeed, they did not even know what was right.

In frustration he turned to the Communicators, because, like the Yackademics and the Civil Serpents, he believed in communications.

Peter Waterhole then appointed an all-powerful regulating agency, run by Harry Boil and seven Frogs from the Shallow End, and told them to reform broadcasting and unite the Swamp.

In case that was not enough, he also instructed the talented and beautiful Jeanne Save-Me to create a new government department called Communications Swamp. She was told to spend a few million more clams to be absolutely sure the animals got the message.

In the end, however, the Communicators could not communicate even with one another, and silently they disappeared one by one into the Swamp.

He was convinced that if he could only communicate at the Ordinary Animals long enough, they would realize how right he had been, and the Swamp would be united.

"It's logical," he said. So he spent a million and a half clams a day on the All Swamp Broadcasting Corporation, but nothing happened. Then one day he asked Michael Pitstop, "Who runs the ABC?"

"No one," replied Pitstop. "It just happens."

Now a befuddled Peter Waterhole turned to the Royal Swampian Mounted Police to see if they could tell him what was happening. The Swampies, you see, were experts at finding things out, having got into the business long, long ago during one of the Swamp's regular postal strikes. At the postal lodge, the mail had been piling up, and it seemed a shame that it should all go to waste, so the Postal Animals decided to read some of it. Well! You wouldn't believe the things they found out!

"We must tell the Swampies," they cried, and rushed off to the police lodge.

At first, the Swampies would not believe them, because nothing much had ever happened in the Swamp and all they had to keep them busy was to sing songs and pose for tourists' pictures. When the Swampies read the letters, however, they realized that terrible things were happening and that action must be taken. "We must notify Nottalot," they cried. "We must alert Commissioner Truncheon."

Just at that moment, another Postal Animal rushed in, bearing in his trembling paws a letter that the Solicitous General himself had written. When they read it, they realized that no one could be trusted, not even the Leaders in Nottalot.

A shocked silence was finally broken by their sergeant saying, "The safety of the Swamp depends on us. We shall work in secret, seeking out the enemies of freedom. No one must be told."

"Not even Commissioner Truncheon?" asked the Swampies.

"Not even Commissioner Truncheon," said their sergeant.

And so the Swampies stopped singing and started opening mail and raiding offices — including those of a publisher in Bullionville who printed disloyal Swamp fables. Finally, as their greatest triumph, the Swampies persuaded their busy little friends the Earwigs to be informers, and the Earwigs called on their friends, and their friends called on other friends, until finally the Swamp was filled with loyal bugs loyally listening to protect democracy.

The Swampies smiled and said, "Freedom will soon be safe." But then some stumble-pawed idiot botched the placing of a bug in the Preservative Party headquarters and, thanks to the irresponsible Press Animals, the Swamp learned all about it.

At first, Peter Waterhole had been annoyed because he had not known how much snooping was going on, but he quickly saw the advantages of the system, and began eagerly listening himself. Even so, he did not learn what was wrong with the Swamp, or what to do about it. He had come to power acclaimed as the Magic Prince, the Wonder Frog, but now he feared that he would be remembered as the leader under whom the Swamp sank.

Desperately he tried to think of something that would reverse the Wallop Pole ratings — named after a pole in the middle of the Swamp where unpopular politicians were taken to be walloped.

He suggested, for example, that they bring the Constitution home from the Land of the Bulldogs.

This idea attracted a few politicians and Communicators, who were interested in that sort of thing, but most animals, it turned out, did not even know that there was a Constitution. Of those who did, most thought that the problem in getting it back was that it was maybe lost in the mail.

"Peter, it won't sell," said Senator Keith Gravy and Jim Costs, the greatest and most brilliant of all the Bag-Animals.

But what else was there?

Peter Waterhole had to think of something because the moment of the Dread Election was drawing ever closer. Frantically, he twisted and turned; so much so that Joe Hoo, who had done absolutely nothing, seemed firm and decisive in comparison.

"What shall I do?" Peter Waterhole cried in anguish one night as he sat alone by the pool at his great lodge in Nottalot in an area called Reedo Falls (a name which bothered Peter because, when translated into Beaver, it came out as Curtain Falls). "What would Mackenzie Sting have done?" he asked.

"Buy them with their own money," said a voice.

Peter Waterhole was so startled that he swallowed several leakers* of water. "W-Who's there?" he demanded, staring wildly as a luminous cloud began to materialize on the edge of the pool.

"Buy them with their own money," chuckled the cloud. "Remember that, my boy, and you'll never go wrong."

"Mr. Sting!" exclaimed Peter Waterhole as the cloud solidified into the unmistakeable dumpy figure of the late Chief Minister.

"Whom did you expect? John Diefenboomer?" said Mr. Sting in some irritation.

"No, well I mean I didn't . . ."

"Be precise, animal, be precise," said Mackenzie Sting. "Eschew obfuscation."

"What I mean is that I *did* buy them with their own money," blurted Peter Waterhole. "But they won't stay bought."

*a unit of measurement in the Confusius scale invented in the homeland of the Frogs. It was introduced to make the Swamp seem more Frog-like.

"Won't stay bought!" exclaimed Mr. Sting. "I won't believe it. In my day, the Ordinary Animals were utterly honest and with a little persuasion remained Gliberal all their lives. Indeed, many continued to vote Gliberal loyally even after they died."

"Today, you can't even be sure how the Bag-Animals will vote," said Peter Waterhole glumly.

Mr. Sting seemed stunned. "I thought I had foreseen every contingency, but it had never occurred to me that the animals could be untrue to a commitment of honour. We'd better talk to C. D. He was my trouble-shooter. C. D., are you there?"

"Fire them all!" came the bellowed reply from the other world. "Fire the Baskers."* Then, in a flash, the glowering figure of C. D. Howl was there before them.

"Clarence, I have always admired your decisiveness, but I don't think it is practicable to dismiss the entire population of the Swamp," said Mr. Sting. "We need further advice. I shall conjure up the Ghosts of Cabinets Past."

The air then filled with unearthly music and the sounds of many voices, and before the astonished eyes of Peter Waterhole there appeared all the Fathers of Conflaberation and the chief members of every cabinet since. In amazement Peter Waterhole began to pick out the faces: Sir John A. MacBeaver, Sir Charles Tippler, Sir Wilfred Laureate, Sir Robert Boredom, Arthur Mean, R. B. Bandit.

Suddenly a flustering, blustering very-much-alive Joey Smallgood splashed down into the chief ministerial pool. "Waterhole, what the hell kind of garden party are you giving?" he exploded. "What am I doing here?"

"I really do not know," admitted Peter Waterhole. "Since you are the only living Father of Conflaburation, I can only assume that Mr. Sting invoked you."

As the Fighting Little Lobster stared about, they all began to talk.

*animals who went south to enjoy the sun while on holiday or on strike.

"The twentieth century belongs to the Swamp!" declaimed Sir Wilfred, thrusting one paw dramatically into his frock-coat.

"And the Swamp wants to give it back," muttered Peter Waterhole.

"The problem's sumple," interjected Sir John A. MacBeaver in a thick accent. "They canna wurk."

"Work!" screeched Mr. Sting. "You're a Preservative reactionary!"

"And you can go to Hull,* said Sir John A., helping himself once again to Peter Waterhole's Swamp Juice.

The voices began to rise and soon it was impossible to tell what anyone was saying.

Finally, as the crowd fell silent, Mr. Sting said, "We simply don't know. We have never experienced anything of this nature. Perhaps we should consult the Press Animals. They have opinions on everything."

Immediately, they were overwhelmed by the roaring sound of the great wooden presses which printed the news of the entire animal world, and before them appeared the two greatest press kings in history, Lord Beavertail and Lord Tom Thumb of Fleece.

"Up the Empire!" cried Lord Beavertail. "Up the Thin Red Line!"

"Up the Bottom Line," said Lord Thumb of Fleece, deftly extracting a clam from Lord Beavertail's pocket.

"Hmmm," said Mr. Sting. "On second thought, perhaps we'd better call on a living intelligence. Who is the greatest genius in your world today?"

"Without question, my friend Prof. John Kenneth Calibrate, the world's greatest master of Ego-Nomics," said Peter Waterhole.

*a terrible place across the river from Nottalot which the Gliberals used as a dumping ground for clams.

"We shall bring him here," said Mr. Sting. Instantly the long, lank, craggy-faced and utterly confused figure of Professor Calibrate skidded in through the bullrushes for a landing.

"Convene the Cuckoothink Conference," he said, when he was calmed down and cleaned up.

The Cuckoothink Conference, of course, was the great Gliberal think-pond at which the destiny of the Swamp had been debated since the beginning of time. Now the greatest of these conferences was proclaimed, and to it came Civil Serpents and Yackademics and Wizards and Hacques and Flacques and Senator Keith Gravy and they all began to think at once.

The sound was deafening, but their combined wisdom was not equal to the problem. "We must have an Almighty Commission," they said finally.

"Our surveys show that the Ordinary Animal isn't big on Almighty Commissions these days," said Keith Gravy. "Let's name half a dozen Unity Task Farces instead."

"Hmmm," said several Civil Serpents simultaneously. "That would increase the infrastructure staffwise by a factor of six. Good thinking."

CUCKOOTHINK
CONFERENCE

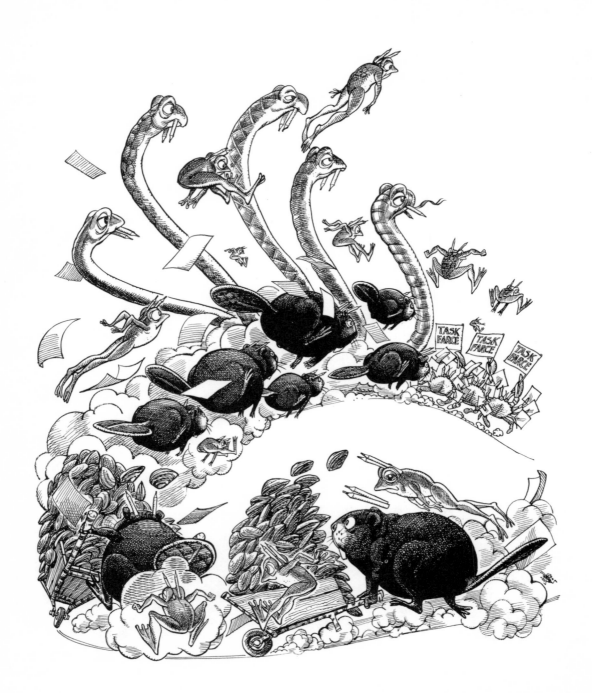

Soon Task Farces in all their majesty were advancing across the Swamp, but alas, after an expenditure of six million words and twelve million clams, they could find no solution.

"We must initiate Permanent Crisis sessions at Nottalot," declared Professor Calibrate.

"In this way we will maximize our top in-house know-how and our best out-house in-put," said the Senior Civil Serpents, flicking their forked tongues wisely.

And so the Great Animals were summoned to Nottalot for the Crisis. There were the great Capital-Nits and the great Bunion Bosses — like Joe More-and-More, who had long led the Swampian Congress of Work, and Joe Dive-in-Son, long an activist — if that is not a contradiction in terms — with the Postal Animals.

Of course all the politicians were there. There were batallions of secretaries banging away at wooden writing machines, and messengers scurrying up and down the tunnels carrying Terribly Important files bulging with birch bark. And there were thousands of Communicators having the time of their lives thrusting forests of wooden microphones in front of Important Animals who said that everything would be fine if only someone else would be reasonable.

In the midst of the Permanent Crisis, Peter Waterhole was finally forced to call the Dread Election, which naturally turned out as everyone had expected.

Peter Waterhole argued logically that, having created the Crisis, he was best qualified to solve it;

Joe Hoo preened his shining new image, prepared specially for the occasion by the most expensive advertising animals in the Swamp;

And Ed Broadlybent of the Trendy Party went from one end of the Swamp to the other crying the timeless cry of the Trendy P, "Time for a Change."

Of course, nothing changed. Except that the Ordinary Animals were getting hungrier than ever.

"Why can't we just go out and catch fish and cut down trees and gather food the way we used to?" they asked.

"But you can't just go to work!" exclaimed the Wizards.

"Work is difficult," said the Yackademics. "If we don't know how to do it, how on earth can you?"

"A threat to the Bunions," said the Bunion Bosses.

"Ridiculous," said the Hacques.

"Dangerous," said the Flacques.

And the Communicators agreed wisely that this was so.

"But wouldn't it be fairer if we all just shared?" said the hungry animals.

"Share!" exclaimed the Wizards. "Share! You don't understand. In the Swamp, everyone is supposed to get rich and you don't get rich by sharing. Be sensible!"

But the Ordinary Animals could not see that it made sense to be hungry when the Swamp was so rich, and they began to sing songs of protest. This made the Bunion Bosses angry. "You can't sing those songs," they shouted. "Those are *our* songs!"

And the politicians and the Civil Serpents and the Wizards and Communicators and Hacques and Flacques told the animals to be patient: the measures being taken to re-float the Swampian economy were almost going to be effective.

But the Ordinary Animals were not patient, and one day some of them simply went to work.

They amazed themselves.

They helped one another, and made friends, and sang together as they worked. And, by the end of the day, they had gathered food, cut down trees, caught fish, and done all kinds of useful things. They were proud of themselves.

They went home at night and told their families, and they were proud and happy too.

So the radical idea spread like wildfire, and soon thousands of animals were happily going to work.

Work was fun.

Work was satisfying.

Work was rewarding.

The "Workers," as these radicals were called, began to say "The Wizards were wrong, and we were right." Some said, "Maybe we don't need the Wizards."

One small voice added: "Maybe we don't need Nottalot."

A silence fell as they pondered this awesome thought. "Perhaps we can do it ourselves," they said finally.

And so conferences were held across the Swamp. The Lobsters met at Hellish-Facts, the Gophers at Win-a-Pig, the Marmots at Call-Girlie, and the Otters at Van Snoozer.

Next a Great Meeting was called to which leaders came from across the Swamp — René Terrifiqué, Big Bill Pave-It of the Beavers, Sterling Lion of the Gophers, Peter Lowspeed of the Marmots, Bill Bendit of the Otters, the leaders of the Turtles and the representatives of the Ordinary Animals.

"Let us run our affairs in the places where we live," they said, "but let us meet from time to time in the Grand Council."

"And let the animals in the Grand Council be the same as those who represent us at home," they said. "In that way, all our representatives will pull together."

It was decided that the Grand Council would meet in succession in all the capitals of the Swamp instead of only at Nottalot.

And it was decided that the Cabinet would consist of leaders from across the Swamp together with the Chief Minister.

Finally it was decided that they really did not need the All-Swamp Broadcasting Corporation and several hundred other Grown Corporations.

Jobs had to be found, of course, for displaced Civil Serpents and Bureau-crabs and Snivel Servants, but since work had become so popular, there were many useful things for them to do.

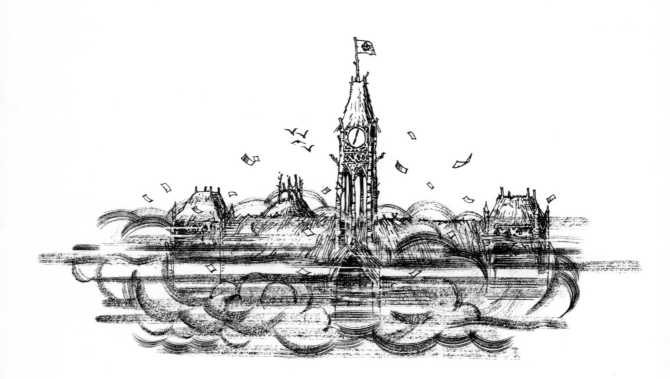

And so it was done, and the animals were delighted.

"This is what we have wanted all along," said the Frogs.

"Finally we are at home in our own land," said the Turtles.

"Now we feel truly part of the Swamp," said the Lobsters and the Gophers, the Marmots and the Otters.

At first the Beavers were uncertain, because they were no longer quite as rich and powerful as before, but when they saw the happiness of the other animals, they too were pleased.

"It will be a better Swamp," they admitted.

In Nottalot, however, the Great Animals remained unaware that anything had happened. So preoccupied were they with the wonderful Crisis that they quite failed to notice when, one night, a group of activist animals quietly cut Nottalot loose and it drifted off into the fog, never to be seen again.

Many say it no longer exists.

Others wonder if it was ever there in the first place.

Some say that, if you get up very early on a still morning, you can sometimes see the towers of Nottalot shimmering in the mist above the Swamp. Some say they have heard shouting and desk-pounding; others have even heard the division bells ringing to summon blissful members to a new and greater Crisis.

And so all the animals were happy and the Swamp was once again prosperous and serene.

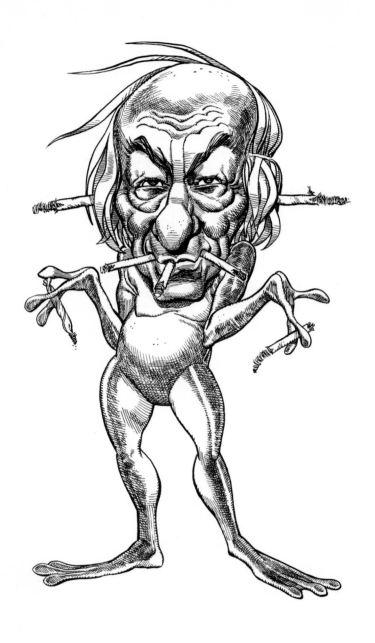

Until they named the new Governor General